Adult Piano Method

Lessons, Solos, Technique & Theory

Fred Kern • Phillip Keveren • Barbara Kreader

Welcome back to the piano! Whether you are continuing from **Book 1** or a student returning to the piano after a break in your study, the music in the **Hal Leonard Adult Piano Method** will excite your interest and imagination. You will find:

- Classical, folk, pop, rock and jazz music with adult appeal
- Realistic pacing that challenges without overwhelming

In addition, you will find:

- **Music Theory** that relates to the music you are playing
- **Technique Tips** that teach you how your physical motions relate to the sounds you want to make
- **Style Clips** that help you with musical interpretation
- **Ad Libs** that teach you how to improvise
- **Quick-Licks** that introduce you to familiar musical clichés so you can sound like a pro right away
- **Sight Reading** tips that help you to read music more fluently
- **Lead Lines** that teach you to improvise an accompaniment

Best of all, each book comes with standard audio and MIDI files, allowing you to play along with an orchestral accompaniment for each piece! Using this model for a polished performance, you will find yourself playing with:

- Increased rhythmic security
- Musical feeling
- Appropriate style

May the **Hal Leonard Adult Piano Method** guide you as you accomplish your life-long goal of learning to play the piano, bringing more music to your life!

Best wishes,

Edited by Alice Brovan

To access audio visit:
www.halleonard.com/mylibrary

4683-9117-2133-9223

ISBN 978-1-4234-2856-5

HAL•LEONARD®
CORPORATION

7777 W. BLUEMOUND RD. P.O. BOX 13819 MILWAUKEE, WI 53213

In Australia Contact:
Hal Leonard Australia Pty. Ltd.
4 Lentara Court
Cheltenham, Victoria, 3192 Australia
Email: ausadmin@halleonard.com.au

CONTENTS

Review of Book One

UNIT 1

Turkish March		6
You Can't Lose with the Blues	*swing tempo, common time* **C**	7
Ad Lib	*five-finger blues pattern*	8
Quick-Lick	*12-bar blues*	8
Dixieland Jam	*semitones*	9
On Cloud Nine	*tones, poco a poco*	10
F Major Pattern	*major five-finger patterns, arpeggios*	11
Midnight Snack Attack	*transposition*	12
Chorale		13
Take It Easy	*chord symbols*	14
Quick-Lick	*creating an accompaniment*	15
Morning Bells	*legato pedalling*	16
Ribbons	*interval of a seventh, simile*	18
Too Good to Be Tuba	*quaver rest*	20
Wayfaring Stranger		22

UNIT 2

Close By	*chords in close position: C Major*	23
Faking It	*lead line in C Major*	24
Beautiful Brown Eyes		24
A Minor Pattern	*minor five-finger patterns*	25
A Minor Tango	*chords in close position: A Minor*	26
Music Theory	*interval reading*	27
Humoresque		28
Related Five-Finger Patterns	*C Major and A Minor*	29
Rustic Dance	*D.C. (Da Capo) al Coda, crossing 2 over 1*	30
Scarborough Fair		31
Lullaby Angel	*Tempo 1*	32
Jig	*3/8, 6/8 time signatures*	34
Two-Four-Six-Eight	*6/8 meter in "2"*	36
C Major Scale	*scale degrees*	38
Key of C Major: Scale and Chord Progressions	*root-position triads, primary triads in C Major*	39
Sight Reading		40
Band on the Beach	*key signature*	41
Changing Lanes	*accidentals*	42
Rondeau		43

UNIT 3

Walking the Beat		44
Relative Scales: C Major and A Minor	*natural and harmonic minor scales*	46
Key of A Minor: Scales and Chord Progressions	*primary chords in A Minor*	47
Allegro		48
Etude	*etude*	49
All the Pretty Little Horses		50
Key of G Major: Scale and Chord Progressions	*primary chords in G Major*	51
Ready to Rock!	*chords in close position: G Major, interval of an octave (8th)*	52
Spanish Dance	*vivace*	53
Song Without Words		54
Faking It	*lead line in G Major*	55
Joshua Fit the Battle of Jericho	*theme and variations*	56
On the Bridge at Twilight	*dim.*	58
Allegro	*cut time* **¢**	60

UNIT 4

Baroque Boogie 62
Etude 64
Blues for a Count . . . . *triplet* 65
Quick-Lick . . . . *Count Basie chord pattern* 66
Related Five-Finger Patterns . . . . *G Major and E Minor* 67
Mister Banjo . . . . *syncopation* 68
On the Prowl . . . . *chords in close position: E Minor* 69
Relative Scales . . . . *G Major and E Minor* 70
Key of E Minor: Scales and Chord Progressions . . . . *primary chords in E Minor* 71
Rhapsody . . . . *tenuto* 72
Wade in the Water 74
Wandering . . . . *adagio* 75
Symphony No. 9 . . . . *allegro con fuoco* 76
Faking It . . . . *lead line in G Major* 77
Style Clip . . . . *the piano as an orchestra* 78

UNIT 5

Related Five-Finger Patterns . . . . *F Major and D Minor* 79
Key of F Major: Scale and Chord Progressions . . . . . *primary chords in F Major* 80
A Pleasant Morning . . . . *allegro moderato* 81
Six Ate Beets 82
Relative Scales . . . . *F Major and D Minor* 84
Key of D Minor: Scales and Chord Progressions . . . . *primary chords in D Minor* 85
Latin Logic 86
A Tender Moment 88
Arabesque . . . . *semiquavers, allegro scherzando, leggiero,* **sfz** 90
The Winter Wind 92
Sight Reading 94
Quick-Lick: Spider Progression . . . . *sequential chord progression* 95
Lyrical Prelude 96
At the End of the Day 98
The Entertainer 100
Für Elise . . . . *poco moto* 102
Appendix: Scales, Chords and Arpeggios 104
Glossary 109
Index 112

THE GRAND STAFF

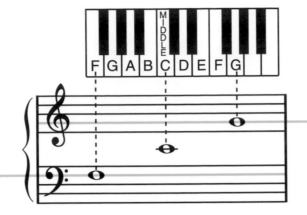

The **G note** is the reading guide
for the **Treble or G Clef** staff (𝄞)

The **F note** is the reading guide
for the **Bass or F Clef** staff (𝄢)

Middle C is the reading guide
for the notes between the Treble
and Bass staves.

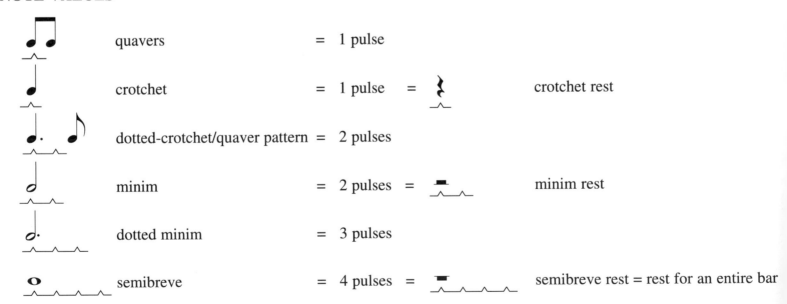

NOTE VALUES

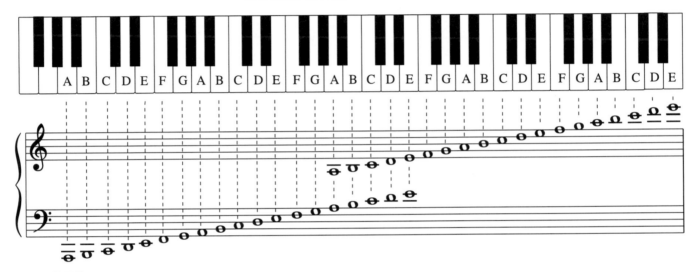

quavers	= 1 pulse			
crotchet	= 1 pulse	= 𝄽		crotchet rest
dotted-crotchet/quaver pattern	= 2 pulses			
minim	= 2 pulses	= ▬		minim rest
dotted minim	= 3 pulses			
semibreve	= 4 pulses	= ▬		semibreve rest = rest for an entire bar

DYNAMICS

pp (*pianissimo*) = very soft

p (*piano*) = soft

mp (*mezzo piano*) = medium soft

mf (*mezzo forte*) = medium loud

f (*forte*) = loud

ff (*fortissimo*) = very loud

< (*crescendo*) = gradually louder

> (*decrescendo*) = gradually softer

An **INTERVAL** is the distance from one key to another.

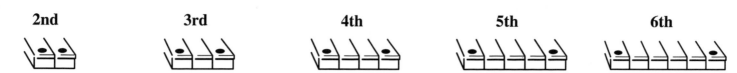

| **2nd** | **3rd** | **4th** | **5th** | **6th** |

FIVE-FINGER PATTERNS

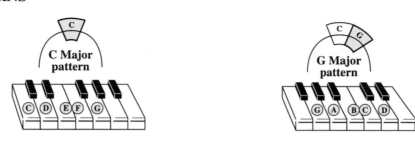

MUSICAL TERMS

time signature	$\frac{4}{4}$ $\frac{3}{4}$	tells how many beats are in each bar and the basic pulse
repeat sign	:‖	play the piece, or sections of the piece, again
legato touch		play smooth and connected
staccato touch		play short and separated
accent		play the note louder
8va/8vb	*8va* - - ⌐	play one octave higher or lower
15ma	*15ma* - - ⌐	play two octaves higher
loco		play the notes where written
a tempo		return to the original tempo
D.C. al Fine		return to the beginning and play to the Fine sign
upbeat(s)		note(s) that come before the first full bar
ritard	*rit.*	slow the tempo
ledger lines		are added to notes written above or below the staff
fermata		hold a note longer than its rhythmic value
phrase		a musical clause or sentence
triad		a three-note chord written on three consecutive lines or spaces

ACCIDENTALS

♯ sharp   ♭ flat   ♮ natural

TEMPO MARKS tell the mood of the piece and the speed of the pulse.

Andante	*Andantino*	*Allegro*
walking speed	slightly faster than Andante	quickly

Turkish March
from THE RUINS OF ATHENS

Ludwig van Beethoven
(1770-1827)
Arranged by Fred Kern

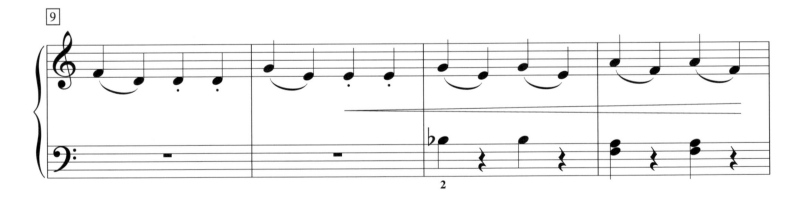

In **"swing tempo,"** quavers are played unevenly.

long   short - long   short - long   short - long   short

You Can't Lose with the Blues

Phillip Keveren

| **An Improvisation Using a Five-Finger Blues Pattern**

You can create a great blues improvisation using these five notes. Improvise as your teacher plays the accompaniment below.

C BLUES PATTERN

Quick-Lick | **12-Bar Blues**

Practise the following blues accompaniment with your left hand. Then, continue to play the accompaniment while you add an improvised melody in the right hand using the C blues pattern.

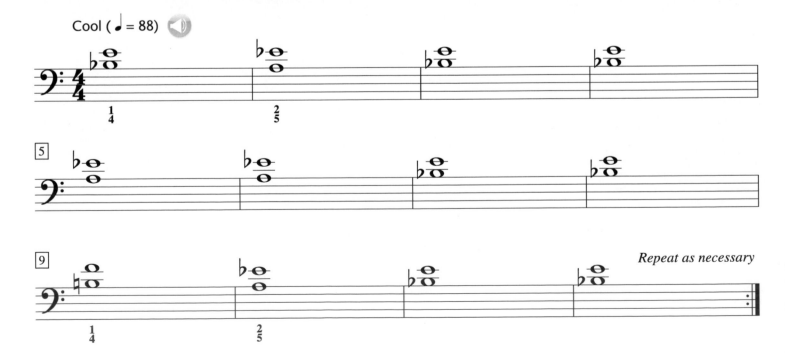

SEMITONES

A **Semitone** is the distance from one key to the next key, either higher or lower, black or white, with no key between.

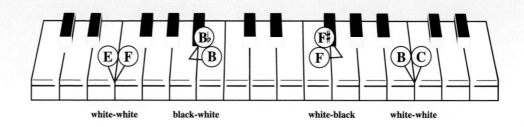

white-white   black-white   white-black   white-white

Dixieland Jam

Bill Boyd

With energy (♩ = 192)
Second time R.H. 8va

TONES

A **Tone** is the distance from one key to another, either higher or lower, black or white, with one key between.

One tone = two semitones

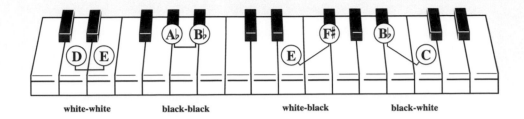

white-white   black-black   white-black   black-white

On Cloud Nine

Mona Rejino

Mysteriously (♩ = 108)

*little by little

MAJOR FIVE-FINGER PATTERNS

All **Major Five-Finger Patterns** are made up of the following series of tones and semitones:

T – T – S – T

ARPEGGIOS

Arpeggios are the notes of a broken chord played one after another, up or down a keyboard. One way to play arpeggios is hand-over-hand.

F Major Pattern

F-G-A-B♭-C

F Major Warm-Up

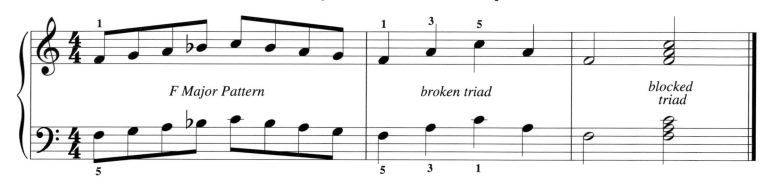

F Major Pattern

broken triad

blocked triad

Technique Tip **Playing Arpeggios**

As soon as you finish playing the last note of the broken triad in bar 1, begin crossing your left hand over your right.

F Major Arpeggio

mf - p

legato

L.H. over

Now play arpeggios using C Major and G Major triads. They are also written out in the Appendix, page 104.

C MAJOR

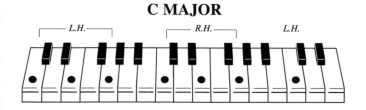

G MAJOR

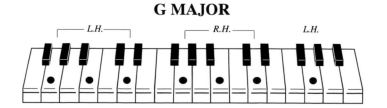

| **An Improvisation (Improv) in F Major**

Place both hands in the **F Major five-finger pattern**. As your teacher plays the accompaniment below, improvise a melody using one hand or the other.

Accompaniment

Midnight Snack Attack

Phillip Keveren

Transposition: *Midnight Snack Attack* is written in the F Major pattern. Place your hands in the C Major pattern and play the piece again. Now **transpose** the piece to the G Major pattern.

Chorale

Fred Kern

CHORD SYMBOLS

Chord Symbols are often written above the treble staff. If a bar does not have a chord symbol above it, the previous chord is continued.

The letter symbol for a major chord is the same as the root of the chord (**C** for C–E–G; **G** for G–B–D; **F** for F–A–C).

Take It Easy

Chord warm-up in root position

Phillip Keveren

Teacher Solo (Play one octave higher than written.)

14

| **Creating An Accompaniment**

1. Play the bass line below with your left hand.
2. Using the letter symbols, play semibreve chords in the right hand.
3. Combine steps 1 and 2.

4. Now play these variations of the Quick-Lick.

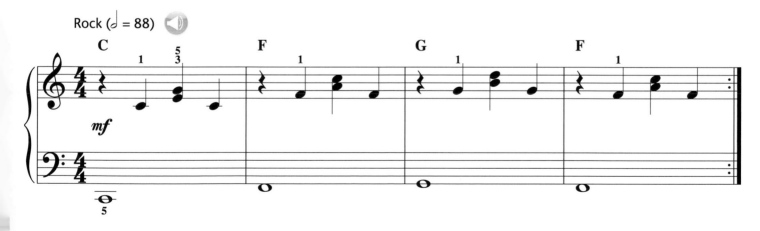

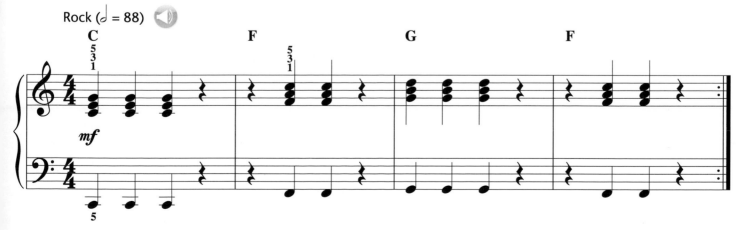

| Technique Tip | **Legato Pedalling** |

First practise pedalling without playing. Place your right foot on the sustain pedal and keep your heel on the floor. Lower and raise the pedal as you count "1 & 2 & 3 &." Use the pedal markings and arrows as a guide.

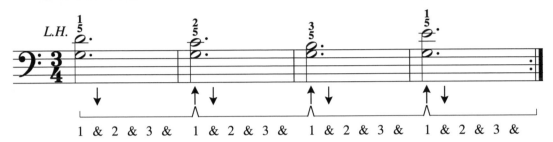

Now play the warm-up below, lowering and raising the pedal as you continue to count the quaver pulse. Using the pedal in this way is called **legato pedalling**.

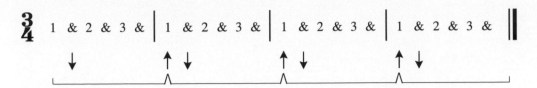

1 & 2 & 3 & 1 & 2 & 3 & 1 & 2 & 3 & 1 & 2 & 3 &

Morning Bells

Phillip Keveren

Brightly ringing (♩ = 138)

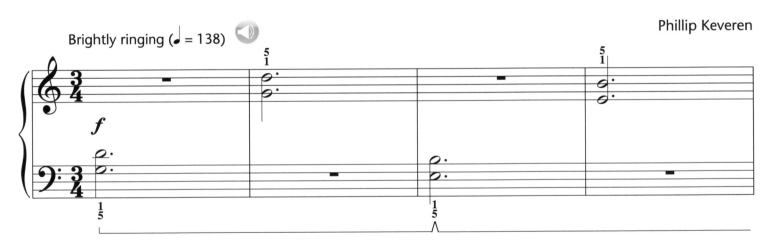

5

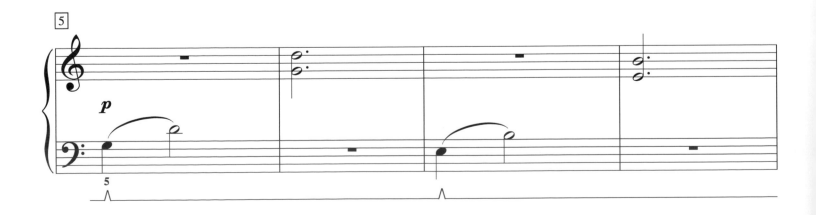

INTERVAL of a 7th

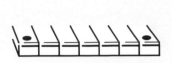

On the piano, a 7th
- skips five keys
- skips five letters

On the staff, a 7th
- skips from either line to
  line or space to space and
  skips five letter names.

Ribbons

Fred Kern

* Continue in a similar manner.

QUAVER REST

A **Quaver Rest** fills the time
of one quaver.

Too Good to Be Tuba

Bill Boyd

Wayfaring Stranger

Spiritual
Arranged by Phillip Keveren

Chords in Close Position
C Major

The notes in root-position chords can be rearranged (inverted) to create closer movement from one chord to the next.

The **G7** chord includes F, the 7th note above G.

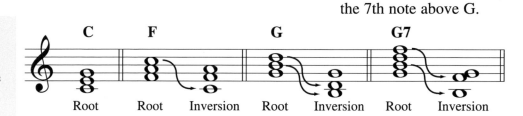

C   F   G   G7

Root   Root   Inversion   Root   Inversion   Root   Inversion

Close By

Phillip Keveren

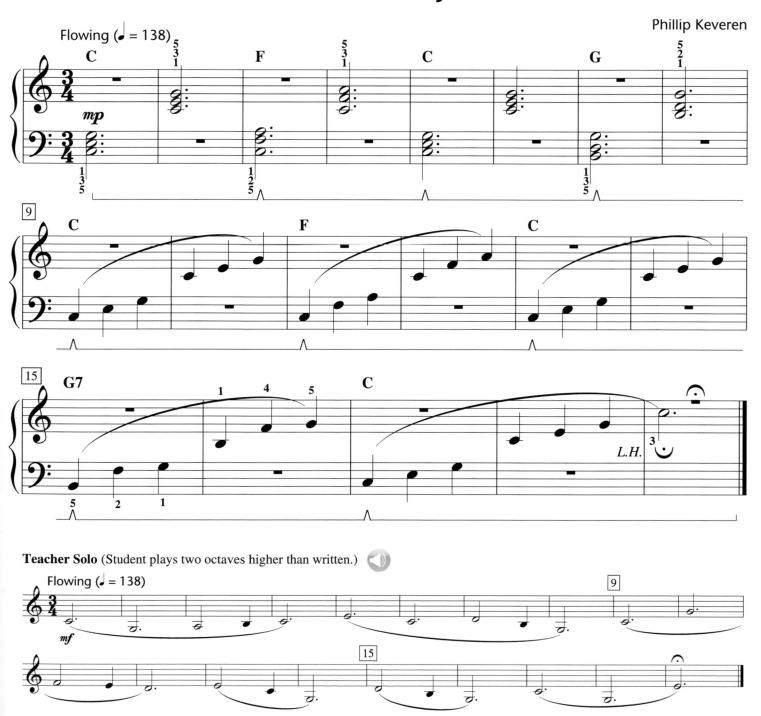

Teacher Solo (Student plays two octaves higher than written.)

Flowing (♩ = 138)

mf

A **Lead Line** of a song consists of the melody, the lyrics, and the chords written in letters above the tune. Pop musicians are required to "fake" (improvise) an accompaniment. A **fake book** is a collection of lead lines and chord symbols.

1. Play the melody "Beautiful Brown Eyes" with your right hand.

Beautiful Brown Eyes

Folk Melody

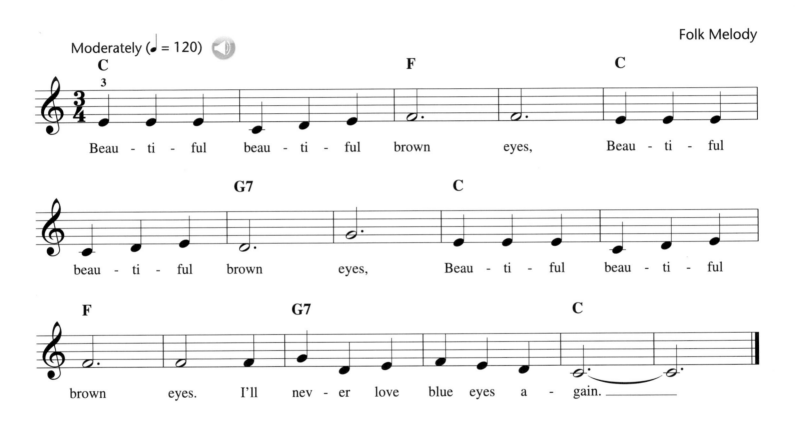

2. Practise the blocked and broken chords below.

3. Create an accompaniment with your left hand using the chord symbols above the melody. You may use a blocked chord or broken chord accompaniment in each bar. If no chord symbol is indicated, repeat the chord of the previous bar.

4. Combine the right-hand melody with the left-hand accompaniment.

A Minor Pattern

A-B-C-D-E

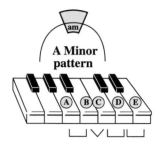

All **Minor Five-Finger Patterns** are made up of the following pattern of tones and semitones:

T – S – T – T

A Minor Warm-Up

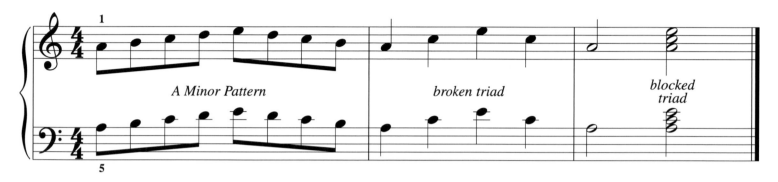

A Minor Pattern   *broken triad*   *blocked triad*

Technique Tip | **Playing Arpeggios**

Listen carefully so you hear no break in the sound when moving from one hand to the other.

A Minor Arpeggio

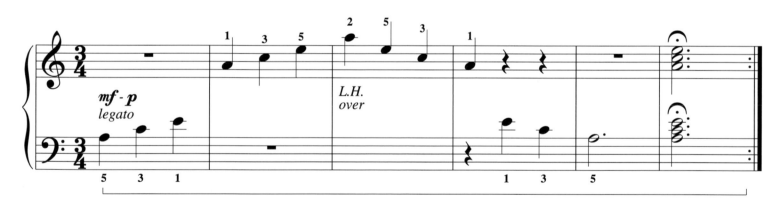

Ad Lib | **An Improvisation Using the A Minor Pattern**

As your teacher plays the accompaniment below, improvise a melody using the A Minor pattern.

Accompaniment (Student improvises one octave higher than shown above.)

Jazzy (♩ = 160)

Repeat as necessary   *Last time*

Chords in Close Position
A Minor

The **E7** chord includes D, the 7th note above E.

Practise these chords in close position before playing *A Minor Tango*:

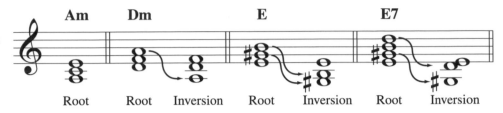

A Minor Tango

Phillip Keveren

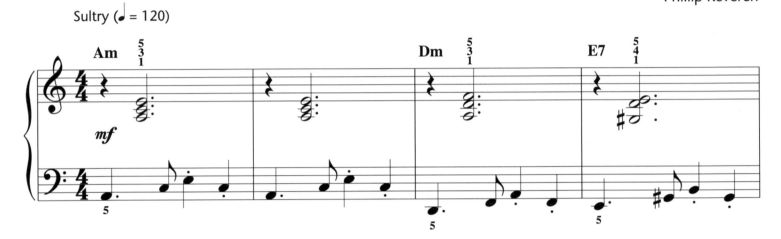

Teacher Solo

Direction, distance, and rhythm are three elements of effective music reading. Use the following steps to organise your approach to fluent reading:

1. Practise the rhythm of each melody by counting the meter and tapping the rhythm with the same hand that will eventually play it.
2. Tap the rhythm and name the intervals by direction and distance.
   a. Say the letter name of the first note, then continue by saying the direction and distance to the next note.
   b. When reading seconds, simply say "up" or "down." (It is not necessary to say "up-a-second.")
   c. When reading intervals larger than a second, say the direction first, followed by the number of the interval, as in the following example:

"C,   up a 3rd, down a 3rd, up a 4th,   up,   down, down, down, down."

Reading and Playing: Finger Taps

1. Tap each melody below in rhythm with the fingers you will use to play each note. Say each finger number as you tap.
2. Repeat, tapping in rhythm and saying the letter name of each note.

Playing and Transposing

Set a tempo by counting two bars. Then play each melody below.

C Major

Transpose to the F Major position.

A Minor

Play this melody in another minor pattern (D Minor) by placing your fifth finger on D.

G Major

Transpose to the C Major position.

F Major

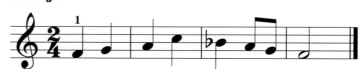

Transpose to the G Major position.

Humoresque

Phillip Keveren

Related Five-Finger Patterns

C Major and A Minor

Every major five-finger pattern has a related minor five-finger pattern.

To find the related minor pattern:
1. Play the major pattern with your L.H.
2. Place your R.H. thumb one tone above the highest note of the major pattern.
3. Play the minor pattern with your R.H.

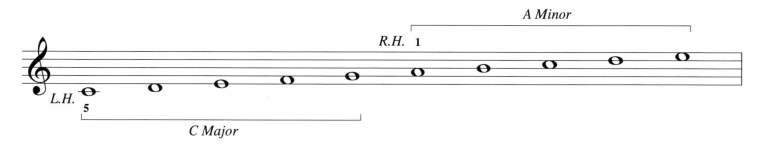

C Major/A Minor Warm-Up

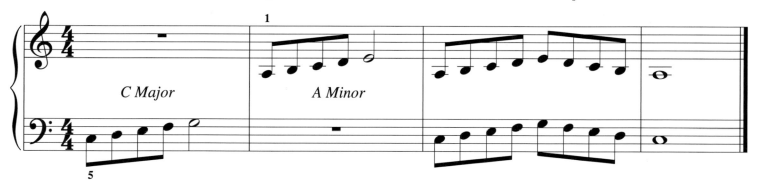

Play the **C Major** and **A Minor arpeggios** in the Appendix, pages 104 and 105.

Ad Lib	**Improvising in C Major and A Minor**

As you listen to the accompaniment, improvise a melody using the C Major pattern with your L.H. and the A Minor pattern with your R.H. Begin playing in the C Major pattern. Your teacher will tell you when to change to the A Minor pattern.

Accompaniment (Student improvises one octave higher than shown above.)

D.C. (DA CAPO) AL CODA

means to return to the beginning
and play to the "To Coda ⊕" sign;
then skip to the Coda and continue
to the end.

Rustic Dance

Barbara Kreader

Scarborough Fair

Traditional English Melody
Arranged by Mona Rejino

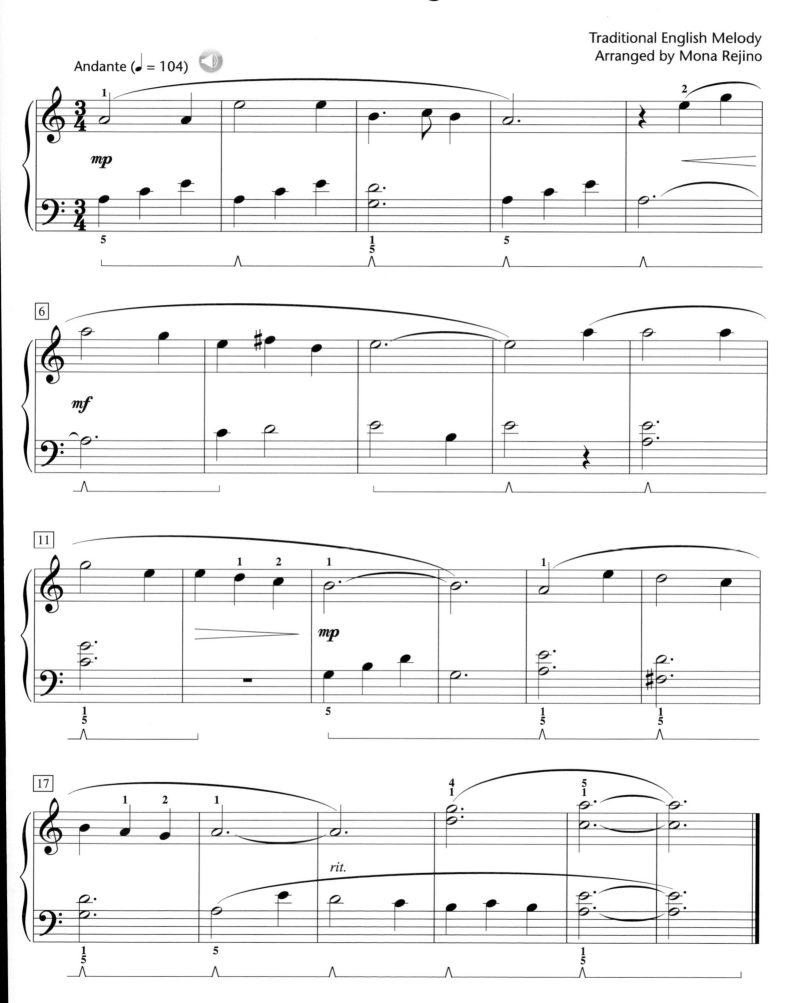

Lullaby Angel

for Lindsay Kay

Phillip Keveren

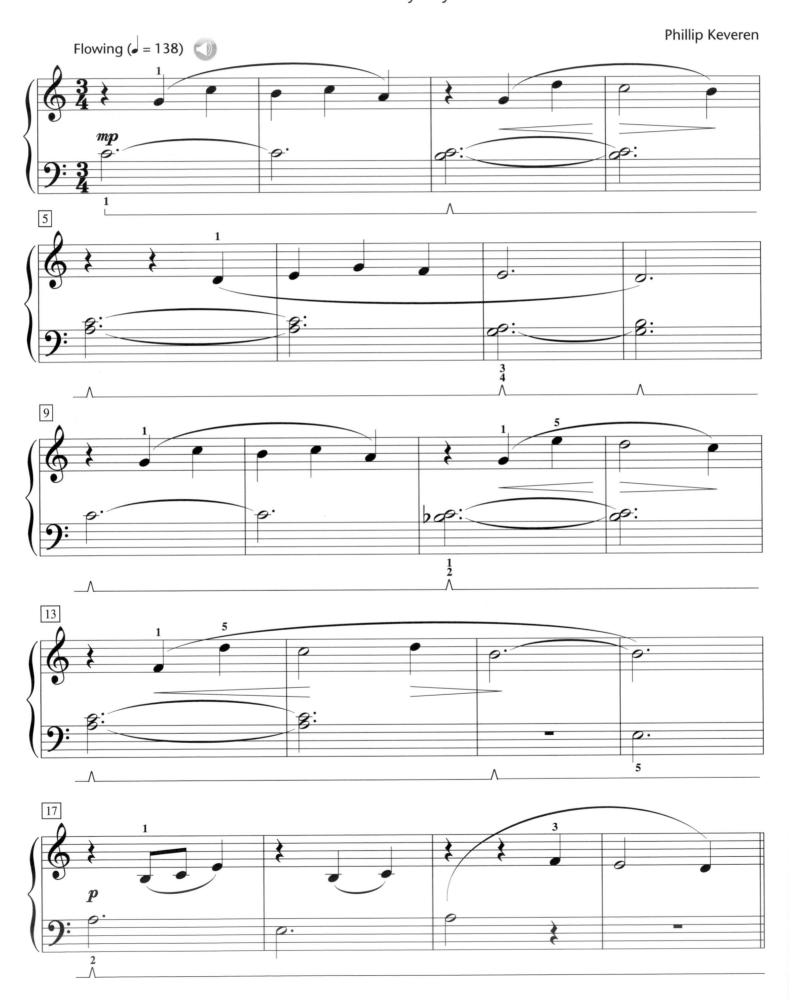

Return to original tempo.

$\frac{3}{8}$ TIME SIGNATURE

$\frac{3}{8}$ (**3**) = three quavers fill every bar
= a quaver gets one beat

Tap and count these patterns:

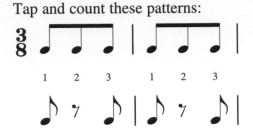

Jig

Irish Melody
Arranged by Fred Kern

$\frac{6}{8}$ TIME SIGNATURE

$\frac{6}{8}$ (**6**) = six quavers fill every bar
$\phantom{\frac{6}{8}}$ = a quaver gets one beat

Tap and count these patterns:

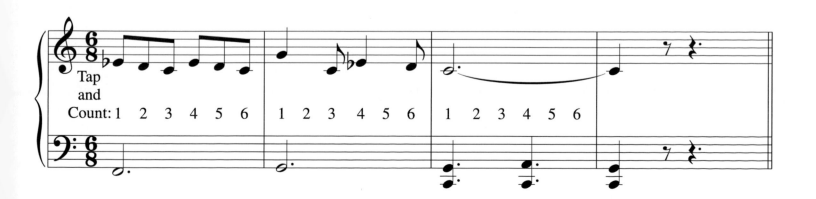

Tap
and
Count: 1 2 3 4 5 6   1 2 3 4 5 6   1 2 3 4 5 6

When a piece in $\frac{6}{8}$ meter is played at a quick tempo, you feel two pulses in each bar.

Count: 1   2   1   2

Two-Four-Six-Eight

Bill Boyd

Jazzy (♩. = 92)

C MAJOR SCALE

All Major Scale patterns are made up of eight notes (degrees) in the following order of semitones and tones.

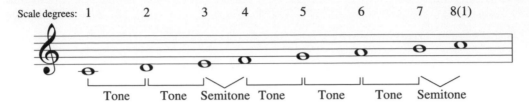

Scale degrees: 1   2   3   4   5   6   7   8(1)

Tone   Tone   Semitone   Tone   Tone   Tone   Semitone

Technique Tip | ## Crossing 3 over 1 and Tucking 1 under 3

When playing scales (R.H. ascending/L.H. descending), tuck your thumb under your third finger. As soon as you play your thumb, move fingers 2-3-4-5 to their new positions.

When playing scales (R.H. descending/L.H. ascending), let your wrist and forearm follow through as you cross your third finger over your thumb. As soon as you play finger 3, move fingers 2 and 1 to their new positions.

Scale Preparation

Smoothly (♩ = 192)

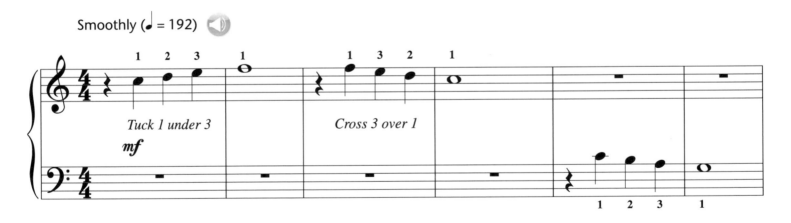

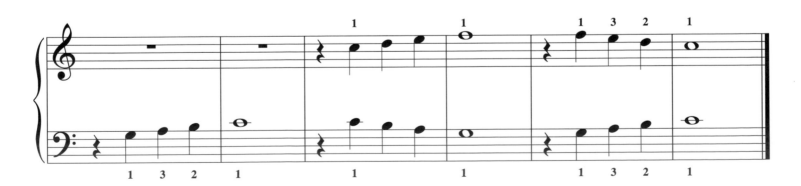

TRIADS IN ROOT POSITION

Root Position Triads can be built on any degree of the scale and are written on three consecutive lines or spaces.

PRIMARY TRIADS (CHORDS)

Triads built on the first, fourth, and fifth degrees of the scale are called **Primary Triads** (or chords). **Tonic (I), Sub-dominant (IV),** and **Dominant (V).**

Key of C Major
Scale and Chord Progressions

The Primary Chords in C Major are:

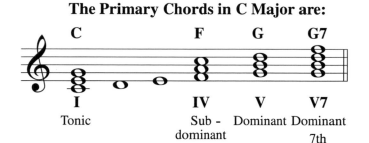

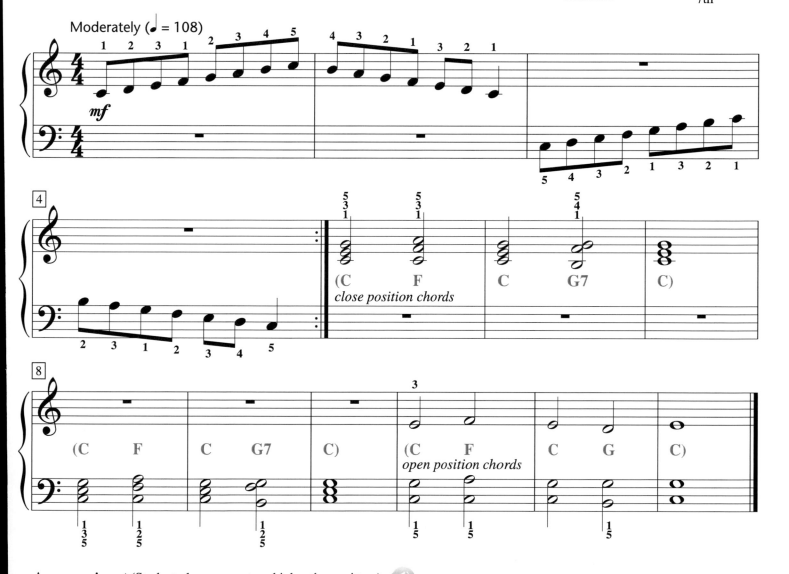

Accompaniment (Student plays one octave higher than written.)

Moderately (♩ = 108)

Sight reading is the simultaneous reading, playing and "performing" of a piece of music *without* practising it.

Steps Before Sight Reading and Playing

1. Observe clef signs and decide where to place your hands.
2. Notice the meter and rhythm; review how to count it.
3. Mentally preview the direction and distance of each interval.
4. Count two bars in a moderate tempo before you begin.

See if you can play the following melodies accurately the first time. Play continuously to the end of each example, even if you have to improvise some notes to maintain the beat.

a.

b.

c.

d.

40

KEY SIGNATURE

Every piece has a **Key Signature** following the time signature.
It identifies the key the composer used and tells you which
notes to play sharp or flat throughout the piece.

Band on the Beach

Key of C Major
Key signature: *no sharps, no flats*

Phillip Keveren

ACCIDENTALS

Sharps (♯), Flats (♭), or Naturals (♮)
added to a piece are called
Accidentals.

Changing Lanes

Carl Czerny
(1791-1857)

Rondeau

Jean-Joseph Mouret
(1682-1738)
Arranged by Fred Kern

Walking the Beat

Phillip Keveren

Relative Scales
C Major and A Minor

Every Major Scale has a **Relative Minor**. It begins on the sixth degree of the Major Scale and shares the same key signature.

A is the sixth degree of the C Major Scale. Therefore, C Major and A Minor are Relative Scales and they share the same Key Signature: *no sharps and no flats*.

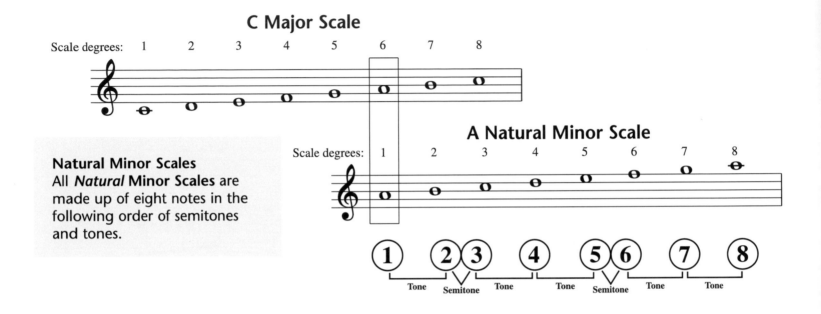

Natural Minor Scales
All *Natural* Minor Scales are made up of eight notes in the following order of semitones and tones.

Harmonic Minor Scales
A *Harmonic* Minor Scale is formed by raising the seventh degree of the Natural Minor Scale one semitone, indicated by an accidental (G♯ in the A Harmonic Minor Scale).

For a quick way to find the relative minor, move down three semitones and three letter names from the first degree of the major scale.

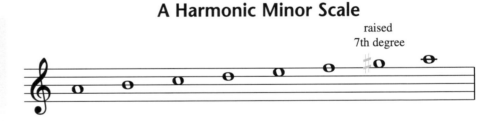

Key of A Minor

Scales and Chord Progressions

The Primary Chords in A Minor are:

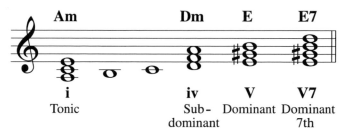

Am	Dm	E	E7
i	**iv**	**V**	**V7**
Tonic	Sub-dominant	Dominant	Dominant 7th

First play the **Natural Minor Scale** with no flats or sharps. On the repeat, play the **Harmonic Minor Scale** with the raised seventh (G♯).

Accompaniment (Student plays one octave higher than written.)

In bars 1-4, play G♮ the first time through; on the repeat, play G♯.

Allegro

Key of A Minor
Key signature: *no sharps, no flats*

Cornelius Gurlitt
(1820-1901)
Op. 82, No. 52

*Etude

Ludwig Schytte
(1848-1909)

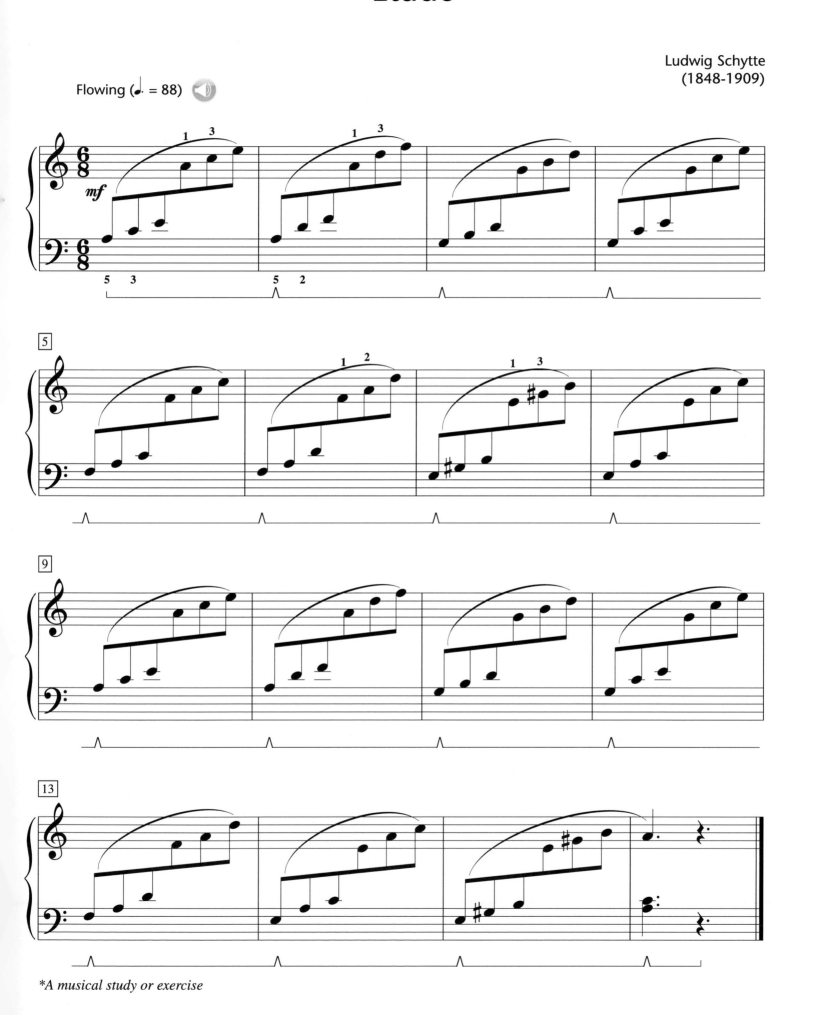

*A musical study or exercise

All the Pretty Little Horses

American Folk Melody
Arranged by Fred Kern

Slowly (♩ = 72)

Key of G Major

Scale and Chord Progressions

The Primary Chords in G Major are:

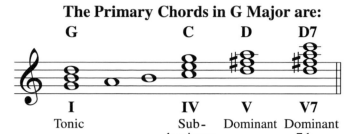

G	C	D	D7
I	IV	V	V7
Tonic	Sub-dominant	Dominant	Dominant 7th

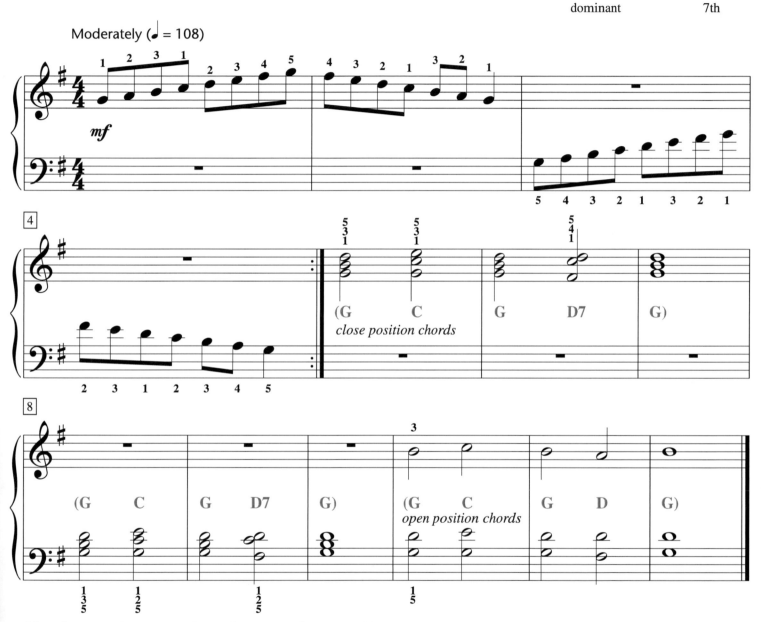

Moderately (♩ = 108)

mf

4

(G   C)
close position chords

G   D7   G)

8

(G   C   G   D7   G)
(G   C
open position chords
G   D   G)

Play the **G Major arpeggio** in the Appendix, page 104.

Accompaniment (Student plays one octave higher than written.)

Moderately (♩ = 108)

mp

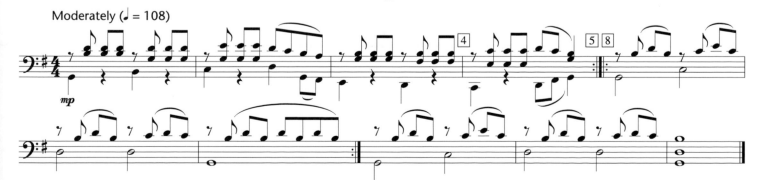

Chords in Close Position

G Major

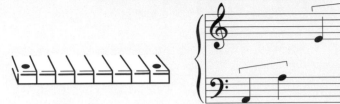

On the piano, an octave
- skips six keys
- skips six letters

On the staff, an octave
- skips six notes, from either line to space or space to line. Both notes in an octave have the same letter name.

Practise these chords in close position before playing *Ready to Rock!*

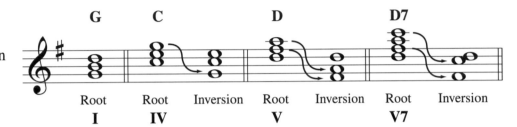

Ready to Rock!

Phillip Keveren

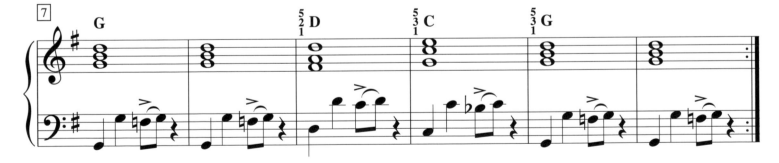

Teacher Solo (Student plays one octave lower than written.)

52

Spanish Dance

Key of G Major
Key Signature: *one sharp, F♯*

Muzio Clementi
(1752-1832)
Adapted by Fred Kern

* Vivace (♩ = 176)

* *Lively*

Song Without Words

Louis Köhler
(1820-1886)
Adapted by Fred Kern

1. Play each melody below with your right hand.

Hush, Little Baby

Folk Melody

Quietly (♩ = 76)

Play R.H. 8va throughout

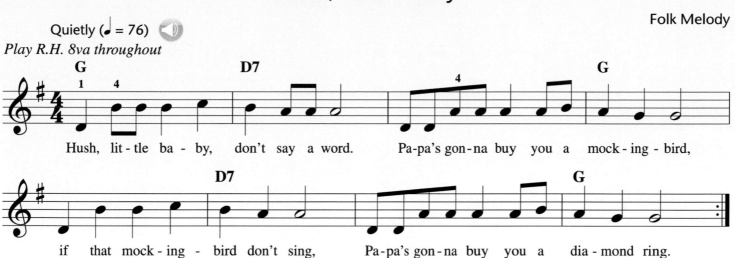

Hush, lit-tle ba-by, don't say a word. Pa-pa's gon-na buy you a mock-ing-bird,

if that mock-ing-bird don't sing, Pa-pa's gon-na buy you a dia-mond ring.

Michael, Row the Boat Ashore

Folk Melody

Flowing (♩ = 88)

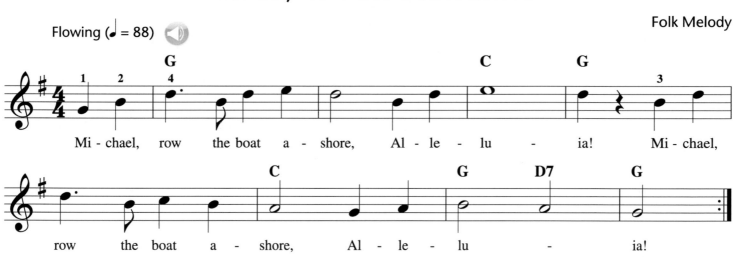

Mi-chael, row the boat a-shore, Al-le-lu-ia! Mi-chael,

row the boat a-shore, Al-le-lu-ia!

2. Practise the left-hand blocked and broken chords below.

3. Now create a left-hand accompaniment for each melody above, using the chord symbols given. Experiment by using either a blocked-chord or broken-chord accompaniment.

4. Combine the right-hand melody with the left-hand accompaniment.

This piece uses a different time signature for the theme and each variation:

$\frac{4}{4}$ for the Traditional style,

$\frac{3}{4}$ for the Classical style,

$\frac{4}{4}$ for the Jazz style.

Joshua Fit the Battle of Jericho
Theme and Variations

Theme: Traditional Style

Phillip Keveren

Variation II: Jazz Style

Laid-back (Swing tempo ♩♩ = ♩ ♪) (♩ = 152)

On the Bridge at Twilight

Jennifer Linn

* Gradually decrease dynamic level.

CUT TIME

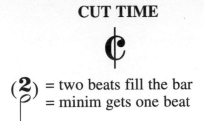

= two beats fill the bar
= minim gets one beat

Allegro
from A LITTLE NIGHT MUSIC

Wolfgang Amadeus Mozart
(1756-1791)
Arranged by Fred Kern and Phillip Keveren

Baroque Boogie
for Sean David

Phillip Keveren

(resume swing)

To prepare to play this piece, block the notes of each three-note grouping. When you play *Etude* as written, drop your arm weight into the first note of each three-note phrase and gradually lift your wrist as you play the second and third notes.

Etude

Jean Baptiste Duvernoy
(1802-1880)

TRIPLET

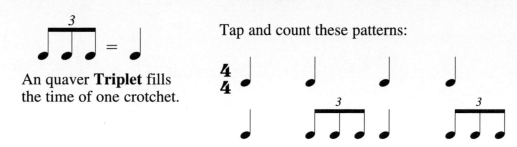

An quaver **Triplet** fills the time of one crotchet.

Tap and count these patterns:

Blues for a Count

Bruce Berr

Count Basie Chord Pattern

You may use the following Count Basie signature chord pattern as an introduction to *Blues for a Count* on page 65. You may also substitute this pattern in bars 15-16 of *Blues for a Count* for a different sound.

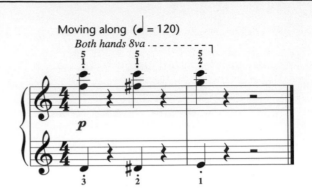

An Improvisation (12-Bar Blues)

1. Play the bass line of the *12-Bar Blues Pattern* below, then write the chord symbol above each bar.

2. As your teacher plays the accompaniment, play the left hand as written and improvise a R.H. melody using the notes in parentheses.

Slowly (♩ = 100)

Accompaniment (Student plays two octaves higher than written.)

Related Five-Finger Patterns
G Major and E Minor

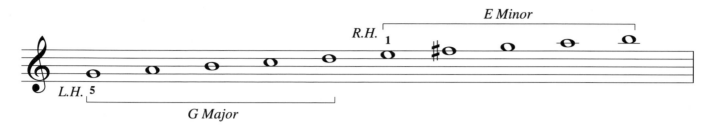

G Major/E Minor Warm-Up

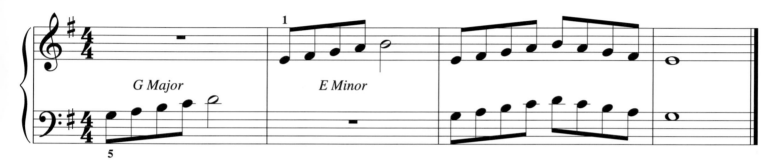

Play the **G Major** and **E Minor arpeggios** in the Appendix, pages 104 and 105.

Ad Lib	**Improvising in G Major and E Minor**

As you listen to the accompaniment below, improvise a melody using the G Major pattern with your left hand and the E Minor pattern (related minor pattern) with your right hand. Begin with the G Major pattern. Your teacher will tell you when to change to the E Minor pattern.

Accompaniment (Student improvises one octave higher than shown above.)

$\frac{2}{4}$ TIME SIGNATURE

$\frac{2}{4}$ ($\mathbf{2}$) = two beats fill every bar
= a crotchet gets one beat

SYNCOPATION

Music becomes syncopated when the rhythmic emphasis shifts to a weak beat—either ahead of or behind the strong beats in the bar.

Tap and count:

Technique Tip | **Syncopation Between Hands**

Tap syncopated rhythms away from the keyboard, saying the hand combinations out loud, either "right," "left," or "together."

Mister Banjo

Creole
Arranged by Phillip Keveren

Chords in Close Position

E Minor

Practise these chords in close position before playing *On the Prowl*:

The **B7** chord includes A, the 7th note above B.

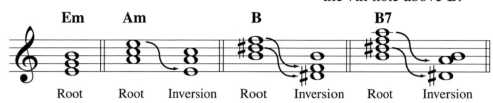

On the Prowl

Phillip Keveren

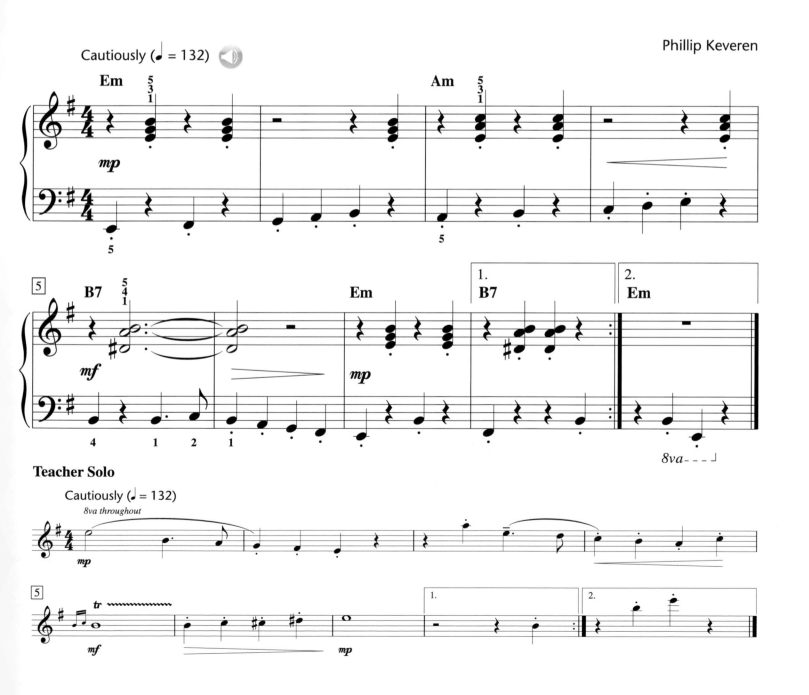

Teacher Solo

Relative Scales

G Major and E Minor

E is the sixth degree of the G Major Scale. Therefore, G Major and E Minor are **Relative Scales** and they share the same **Key Signature**: *one sharp, F♯.*

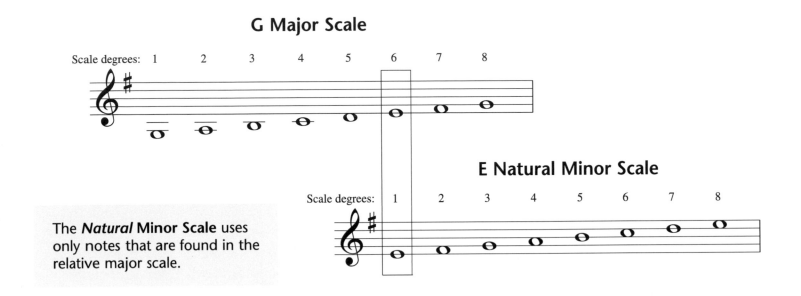

The *Natural* **Minor Scale** uses only notes that are found in the relative major scale.

E Harmonic Minor Scale

The *Harmonic* **Minor Scale** is formed by raising the seventh degree one semitone, indicated by an accidental (D♯ in the E Harmonic Minor Scale).

Key of E Minor
Scales and Chord Progressions

The Primary Chords in E Minor are:

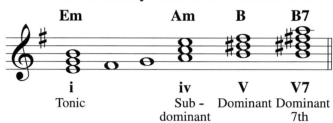

First, play the **Natural Minor Scale** with the F♯ only. On the repeat, play the **Harmonic Minor Scale** with the raised seventh (D♯).

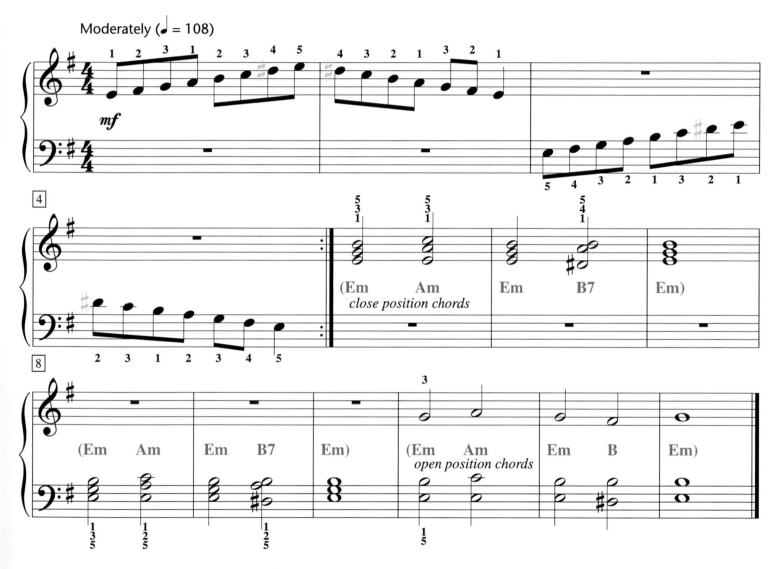

Accompaniment (Student plays one octave higher than written.)

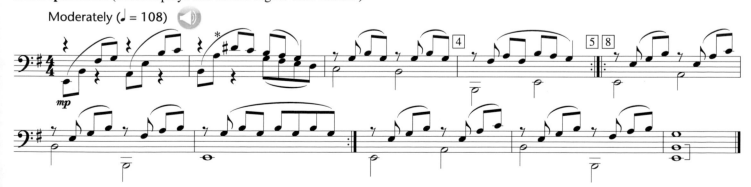

In bars 1-4, play D♮ the first time through; on repeat, play D♯.

TENUTO

A short line over $\overline{\mathsf{f}}$ or under $\underline{}$ a note means to play **Tenuto**. Give the note extra emphasis, holding it for its full value.

Rhapsody

Key of E Minor
Key signature: *one sharp, F♯.*

Jennifer Linn

Tap and count:

Wade in the Water

African-American Spiritual
Arranged by Fred Kern

Tap and count these patterns:

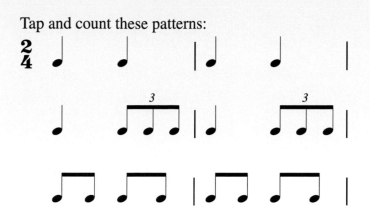

Wandering

Fred Kern

* Adagio (♩ = 72)

* Slowly

Symphony No. 9
Fourth Movement Theme

Antonín Dvořák
(1841-1904)
Arranged by Phillip Keveren

* Allegro con fuoco (♩ = 138)

*Fast, with fire

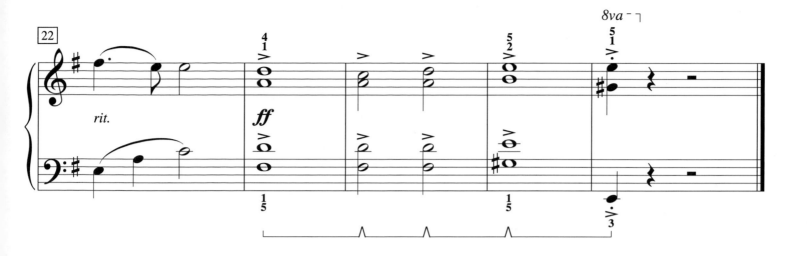

Style Clip | **Nationalism in Music**

The Czech composer Antonín Dvořák (1841-1904) was one of the figures most identified with nationalism in music, a movement that began in the late-Romantic era that was characterized in part by the incorporation of folk tunes into art songs, chamber music, symphonic works, and operas. His *Symphony No. 9*, "From the New World," evokes the spirit and style of African-American spirituals and Native American songs. Dvořák wrote his *Symphony No. 9* after he had visited America in the late 1800s. An American, William Arms Fisher (1861-1948), later added lyrics to the tender melody found in the second movement. This theme has remained immensely popular, and it is often heard today as the song "Goin' Home."

Faking It | **Lead Line in G Major**

1. Play the melody to *Goin' Home* with your right hand.
2. Using the chord symbols as a guide, practise the chord progression in blocked chords in your left hand.
3. Create an accompaniment, referring to page 55 for some examples of blocked- and broken-chord styles.
4. Combine the R.H. melody with the L.H. accompaniment.

Symphony No. 9
Second Movement Theme

Music by Antonín Dvořák

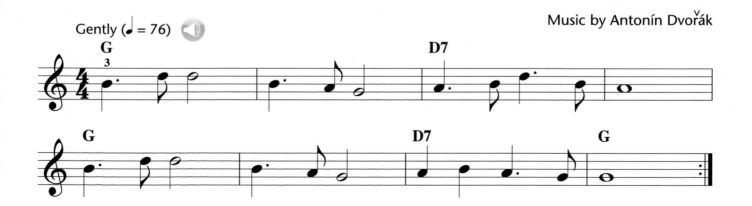

The Piano as an Orchestra

The piano, with its wide tonal range and rich sonorities, can evoke the colours of an entire orchestra. Composers imitate various instruments when employing the appropriate

- Range: the pitch area where the instruments normally play
- Articulation: e.g., *staccato*, *legato*, accent, etc.
- Voicing: the proper pitch to fit the instrument's character of sound

Listen as your teacher plays the Style Clip below.

Phillip Keveren

Related Five-Finger Patterns

F Major and D Minor

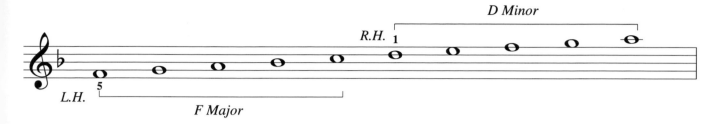

F Major/D Minor Warm-Up

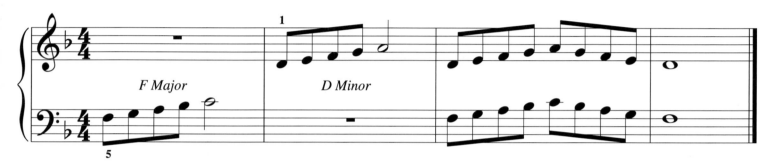

Play the **F Major** and **D Minor arpeggios** in the Appendix, pages 106 and 107.

Ad Lib	Improvising in F Major and D Minor

As you listen to the accompaniment below, improvise a melody using the F Major pattern with your left hand and the D Minor pattern (related minor pattern) with your right hand. Begin with the F Major pattern. Your teacher will tell you when to change to the D Minor pattern.

Accompaniment (Student improvises one octave higher than shown above.)

Key of F Major
Scale and Chord Progressions

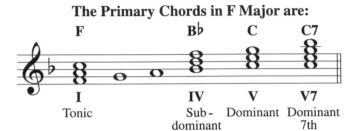

The Primary Chords in F Major are:

F	B♭	C	C7
I	IV	V	V7
Tonic	Sub-dominant	Dominant	Dominant 7th

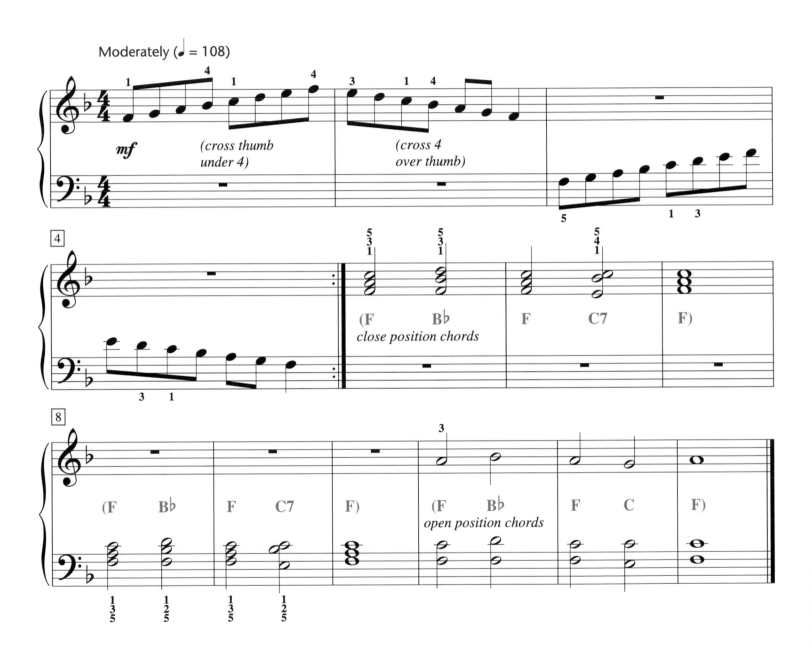

Moderately (♩ = 108)

mf

(cross thumb under 4)

(cross 4 over thumb)

(F   B♭   F   C7   F)
close position chords

(F   B♭   F   C7   F)

(F   B♭   F   C   F)
open position chords

Accompaniment (Student plays one octave higher than written.)

Moderately (♩ = 108)

mp

A Pleasant Morning

Louis Streabbog
(1835-1886)
Opus 63, No. 1
Adapted by Fred Kern

Key of F Major

Key signature: *one flat, B♭*

* Allegro moderato (♩ = 120)

* *Moderately fast*

Six Ate Beets

Bill Boyd

Relative Scales
F Major and D Minor

D is the sixth degree of the F Major Scale. Therefore, F Major and D Minor are **Relative Scales** and they share the same **Key Signature:** *one flat, B♭.*

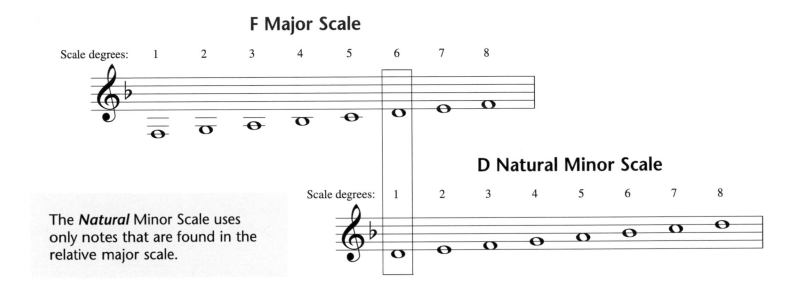

The *Natural* Minor Scale uses only notes that are found in the relative major scale.

The *Harmonic* Minor Scale is formed by raising the seventh degree one semitone, indicated by an accidental (C♯ in the D Harmonic Minor Scale).

Key of D Minor
Scales and Chord Progressions

The Primary Chords in D Minor are:

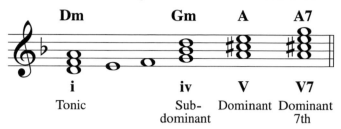

First, play the **Natural Minor Scale** with the B♭ only. On the repeat, play the **Harmonic Minor Scale** with the raised seventh (C♯).

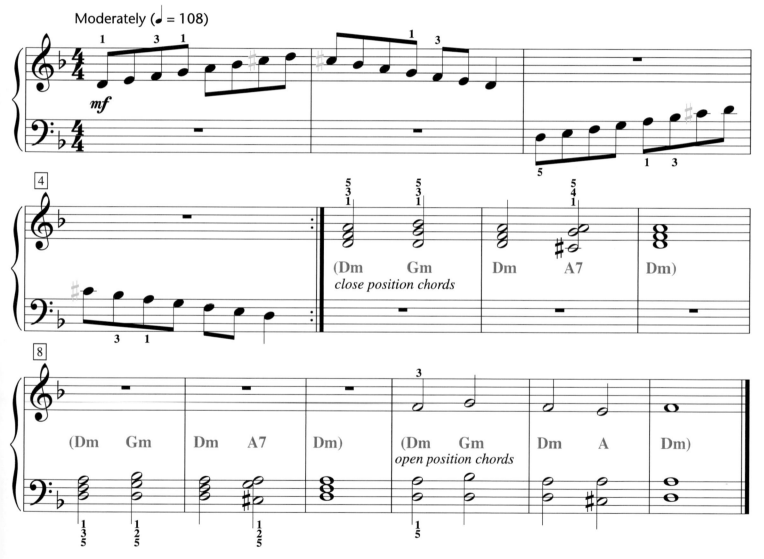

Accompaniment (Student plays one octave higher than written.)

In bars 1-4, play C♮ the first time through; on repeat, play C♯.

85

Latin Logic

Key of D Minor

Key signature: *one flat, B♭*

Bill Boyd

Moderate Latin Rock (♩ = 138)

A Tender Moment

Four **Semiquavers** fill the time of
one crotchet.

Tap and count these patterns:

Arabesque

J. Fredrich Burgmüller
(1806-1874)

Allegro scherzando * (♩ = 104)

*Playfully   ** Lightly
*** Sudden strong accent

The Winter Wind

Carol Klose

Sight Reading

Select a comfortable tempo for each of the following exercises and play them continuously to the end, even if you have to improvise some notes to maintain the beat.

1. C Major

(Transpose to G Major)

2. G Major

(Transpose to F Major)

3. E Minor

(Transpose to D Minor)

4. F Major

(Transpose to C Major)

5. D Minor

(Transpose to A Minor)

Spider Progression

This sequential chord progression occurs as a unifying element in music from classical to popular styles. Listen for similar chord progressions in *Lyrical Prelude* on page 96.

Smoothly (♩ = 84)

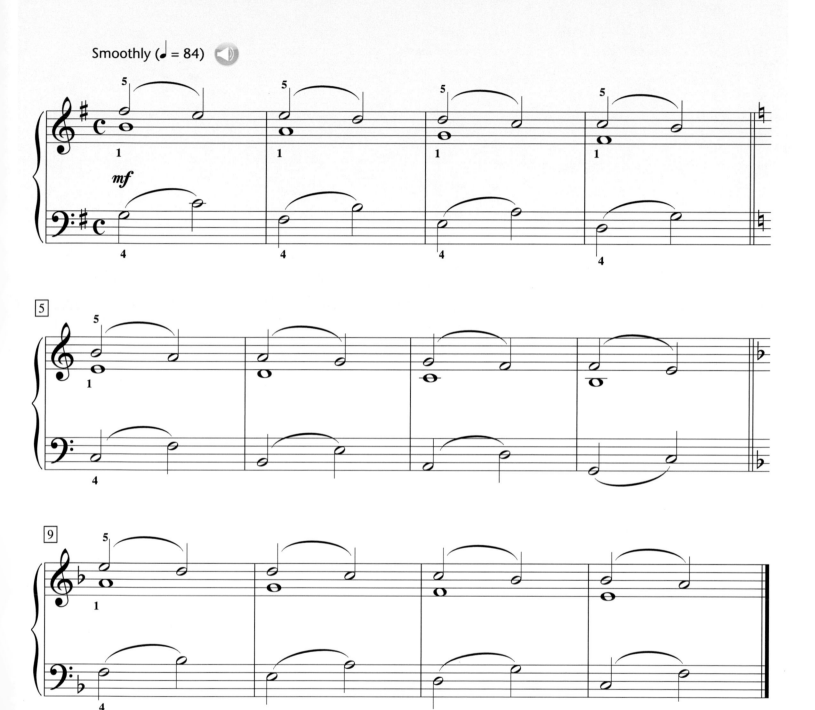

Lyrical Prelude

Phillip Keveren

At the End of the Day

for my Dad

Fred Kern

The Entertainer

Scott Joplin
(1868-1917)
Arranged by Mona Rejino

100

101

Tap and count these patterns:

Für Elise

Ludwig van Beethoven
(1770-1827)
Adapted by Fred Kern

* Moving along

*In some editions, this note is an E, as in bars 7 and 15.

Major Scales, Primary Chords, and Cross-Hand Arpeggios

Play each scale:
- R.H. and L.H. alone
- Hands together

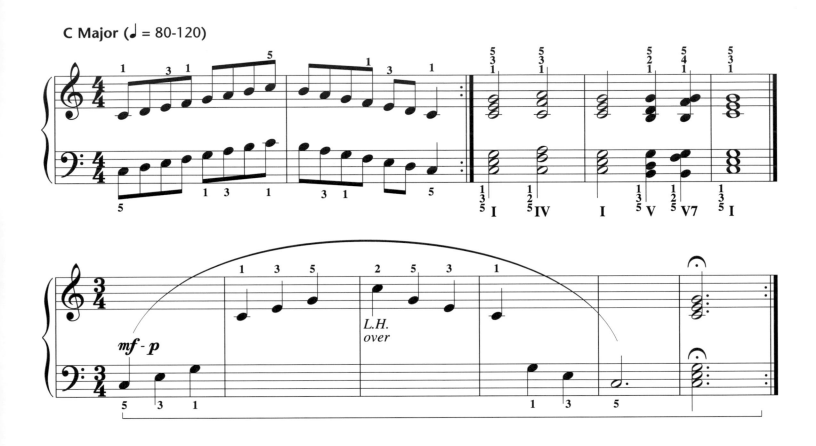

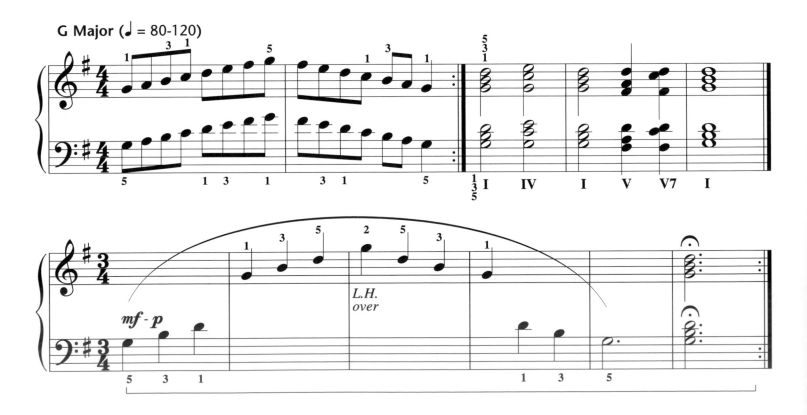

Minor Scales, Primary Chords, and Cross-Hand Arpeggios

First, play the **Natural Minor Scale**. On the repeat, play the **Harmonic Minor Scale**, adding the raised 7th degree.

Play each scale:
- R.H. and L.H. alone
- Hands together

A Minor (♩ = 80-120)

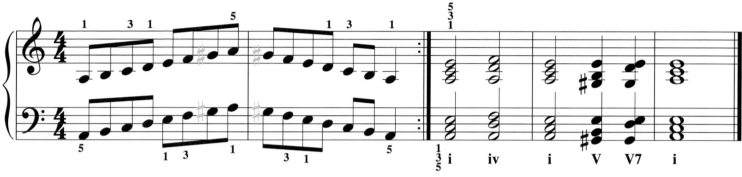

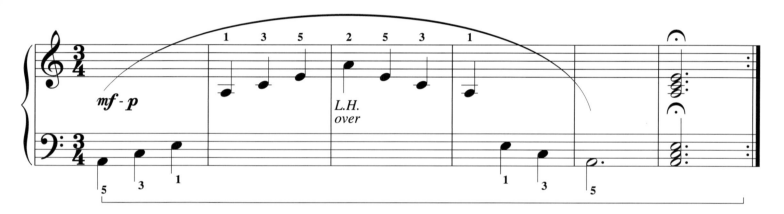

E Minor (♩ = 80-120)

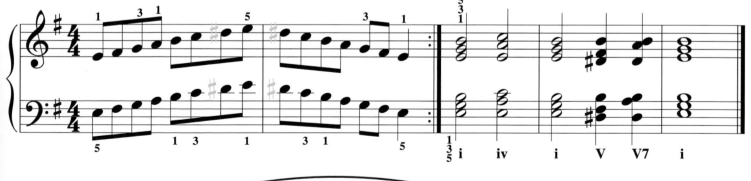

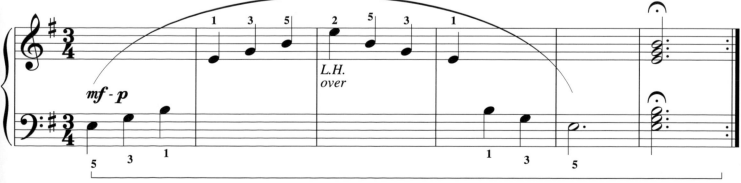

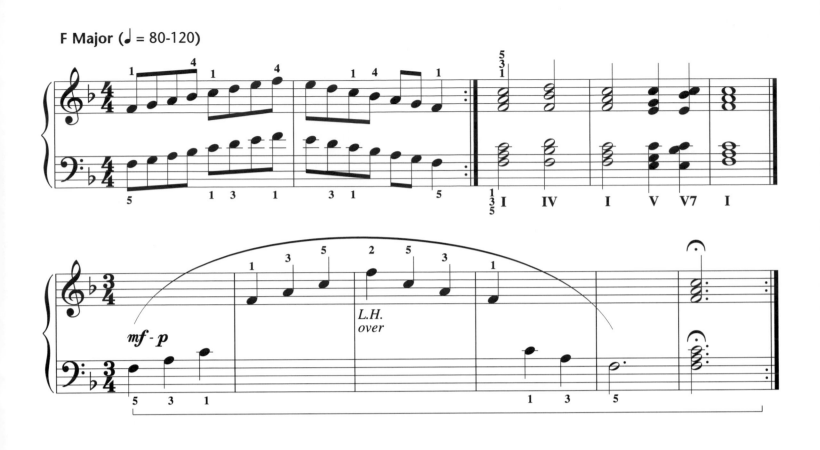

F Major (♩ = 80-120)

Two-Octave Major Scales

After learning one-octave Major and Minor scales, expand your technical skills by practising **Two-Octave Scales**, as shown below. The R.H. fingerings are above the notes; the L.H. fingerings are below. Always play the L.H. one octave lower.

Play each scale:
- R.H. and L.H. alone
- Hands together
- (♩ = 60-80)

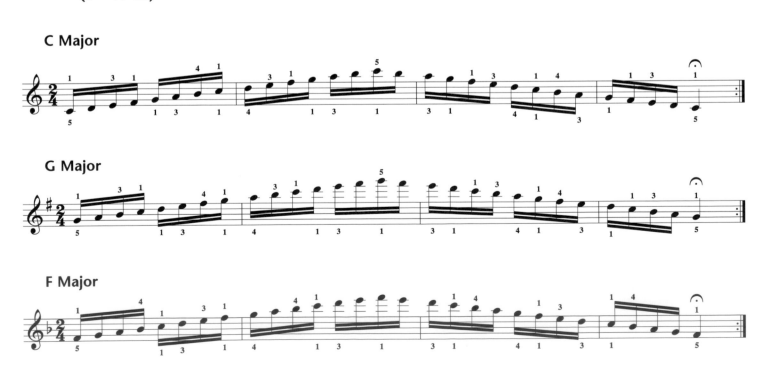

C Major

G Major

F Major

D Minor (♩ = 80-120)

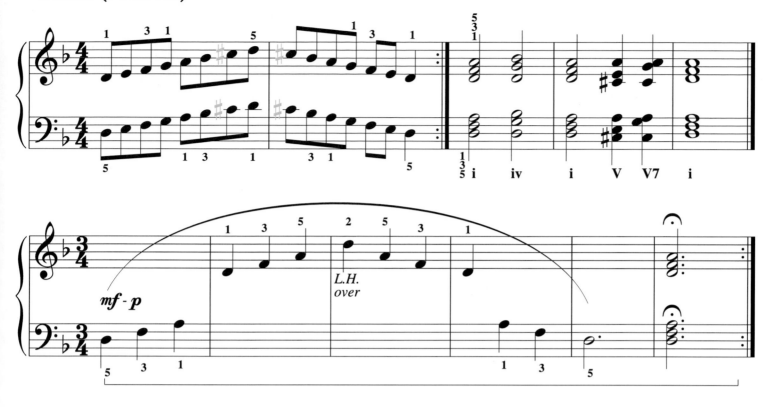

i   iv   i   V   V7   i

Two-Octave Minor Scales

First, play the **Natural Minor Scale**. On the repeat, play the **Harmonic Minor Scale**, adding the raised 7th degree.
Always play the L.H. one octave lower.

Play each scale:
- R.H. and L.H. alone
- Hands together
- (♩ = 60-80)

A Minor

E Minor

D Minor

Circle of Fifths

Beginning with C and moving counter-clockwise around the Circle of Fifths, the order of flat keys is:

C F B♭ E♭ A♭ D♭ G♭ C♭

Beginning with C and moving clockwise around the Circle of Fifths, the order of sharp keys is:

C G D A E B F♯ C♯

Every key signature stands for a major key or its relative minor key. Relative minor keys start on the sixth degree of the major key and use the same notes.

The order in which FLATS occur in a key signature is:

B♭ E♭ A♭ D♭ G♭ C♭ F♭

The order in which SHARPS occur in a key signature is:

F♯ C♯ G♯ D♯ A♯ E♯ B♯

3/8 Time Signature $\begin{smallmatrix}3\\8\end{smallmatrix}$	Three beats fill every bar and a quaver gets one beat.
6/8 Time Signature $\begin{smallmatrix}6\\8\end{smallmatrix}$	Six beats fill every bar and a quaver gets one beat.
2/4 Time Signature $\begin{smallmatrix}2\\4\end{smallmatrix}$	Two beats fill every bar and a crotchet gets one beat.
3/4 Time Signature $\begin{smallmatrix}3\\4\end{smallmatrix}$	Three beats fill every bar and a crotchet gets one beat.
4/4 Time Signature $\begin{smallmatrix}4\\4\end{smallmatrix}$	Four beats fill every bar and a crotchet gets one beat.
8va/8vb/Loco	When the sign *8va* appears over or under a note or a group of notes, play the note or notes one octave higher or lower than written. *8vb* means to play one octave lower. *Loco* means to play the notes where they are written.
15ma	When the sign *15ma* appears over or under a note or group of notes, play the notes two octaves higher or lower than written.
A tempo	*A tempo* means to return to the original speed.
Accent	An **Accent** over or under a note means to play that note louder.
Accidentals	Sharps (♯), flats (♭), or naturals (♮) added to a piece are called **Accidentals**.
Adagio	*Adagio* is a slow tempo, slower than *Andante*.
Allegro	*Allegro* means a quick, lively tempo.
Allegro Con Fuoco	*Allegro Con Fuoco* means to play "fast, with fire."
Allegro Moderato	*Allegro Moderato* is a tempo slightly slower than *Allegro*.
Andante	*Andante* indicates a relaxed, walking tempo.
Andantino	*Andantino* is a slightly faster tempo than *Andante*.
Arpeggios	**Arpeggios** are the notes of a broken chord played one after another, up or down the keyboard.
Chords in Close Position	When the notes in root-position triads are re-arranged (inverted) to create closer movement from one chord to the next, they are called **Chords in Close Position**.
Chord Symbols	**Chord Symbols** are often written above the treble staff. They identify the chord that is played. The letter symbol for a major chord is the same as the root of the chord. (C for C-E-G; G for G-B-D; F for F-A-C.)
Common Time C	**Common Time** is another name for 4/4.
Crescendo (cresc.)	*Crescendo* means to play gradually louder.
Cut Time ¢	In **Cut Time** [¢], two beats fill every bar and a minim gets one beat.
D.C. (Da Capo) al Coda and **"To Coda [⊕]"**	**D.C. al Coda** means to return to the beginning and play to the "To Coda [⊕]" sign; then skip to the Coda and continue to the end.
Da Capo al Fine	**D.C. (Da Capo) al Fine** means to return to the beginning and play to the **Fine** sign.
Decrescendo *Diminuendo* (*dim.*)	*Decrescendo* and *Diminuendo* (*dim.*) mean to gradually decrease the dynamic level.
Etude	An **Etude** is a musical study or exercise.
Fermata 𝄐	A *Fermata* means to hold the note longer than its rhythmic value.

Flat ♭	A **Flat** sign before a note means to play that note one semitone lower, whether black or white. When a flat appears before a note as an **accidental**, it remains flat for the entire bar.
Forte *f*	*Forte* means to play loudly.
Fortissimo *ff*	*Fortissimo* means to play very loudly.
Harmonic Minor Scales	A **Harmonic Minor Scale** is formed by raising the seventh degree of the **Natural Minor Scale** one semitone, indicated by an accidental.
Interval of a 7th	A **7th** skips five keys on the piano, and skips five letters. On the staff, a **7th** skips from either line to line or space to space and skips five letter names.
Interval of an Octave (8th)	An **Octave (8th)** skips six keys on the piano, and skips six letters. On the staff, an **Octave** skips six notes, from either line to space or space to line. Both notes in an **Octave** have the same letter name.
Key Signature	Every piece has a **Key Signature** following the time signature. It identifies the key the composer used and tells you which notes to play sharp or flat throughout the piece.
Lead Line/Fake Book	A **Lead Line** of a song consists of the melody, the lyrics, and the chords written in letters above the tune. A **Fake Book** is a collection of lead lines and chord symbols.
Legato	*Legato* indicates smooth and connected playing with no break in the sound.
Legato Pedalling ⌄⌄⌄	**Legato Pedalling** connects notes or chords in a smooth, unbroken line.
Leggiero	*Leggiero* means to play lightly.
Major Scales	All **Major Scale** patterns are made up of eight notes (degrees) in the following order of semitones and tones: **T – T – S – T – T – T – S**
Mezzo Forte	*Mezzo Forte* means to play moderately loud.
Mezzo Piano	*Mezzo Piano* means to play moderately soft.
Natural ♮	A **Natural** sign cancels a sharp or a flat.
Natural Minor Scales	All **Natural Minor Scales** are made up of eight notes in the following order of tones and semitones: **T – S – T – T – S – T – T**
Phrase	A **Phrase** is a musical clause or sentence. **Slurs** often divide music into phrases.
Piano *p*	*Piano* means to play softly.
Pianissimo *pp*	*Pianissimo* means to play very softly.
Poco a poco	*Poco a poco* means "little by little."
Poco Moto	*Poco Moto* means "moving along."
Primary Triads (Chords)	Triads built on the first, fourth, and fifth degrees of the scale are called **Primary Triads** or **Primary Chords**. They are labeled Tonic (**I**), Sub-Dominant (**IV**), and Dominant (**V** or **V7**).
Quaver Rest ♪	A **Quaver Rest** fills the time of one quaver.
Relative Scales	Every Major Scale has a **Relative Minor**. It begins on the sixth degree of the Major Scale and shares the same key signature.
Repeat Sign :‖	A **Repeat Sign** means play the piece, or sections of the piece, again.
Ritard (rit.)	*Ritard (rit.)* means to slow the tempo gradually.
Root Position Triads	**Root Position Triads** can be built on any degree of the scale and are written on three consecutive lines or spaces (C – E – G).

Scherzando	*Scherzando* means "playfully."
Semiquavers	Four **Semiquavers** fill the time of one crotchet.
Semitone	A **Semitone** is the distance from one key to the next key, higher or lower, black or white, with no key in between.
Seventh Chords	A **Seventh Chord** includes the 7th note above the root. (G – B – D – F). In root position, the number 7 is added to the chord symbol (**C7, G7, F7**).
Sforzando *sfz*	*Sforzando* means to play a note or chord with a sudden, strong accent.
Sharp ♯	A **Sharp** sign before a note means to play the note one semitone higher, whether black or white. When a sharp appears before a note as an **accidental**, it remains sharp for the entire bar.
Simile	*Simile* means to continue in the same manner.
Slur	A **Slur** is a curved line over or under a group of notes that means to play *legato*.
Staccato	A dot over or under a note means to play the note *Staccato* – short and detached.
Sustain Pedal	The **Sustain Pedal** releases the dampers from the strings, causing the sound to vibrate longer.
Swing Tempo	**Swing Tempo** quavers are played unevenly and are found often in pieces in jazz style.
Syncopation	Music becomes **syncopated** when the rhythmic emphasis shifts to a weak beat – either ahead of, or behind the strong beats in the bar.
Tempo I	**Tempo I** means return to the original tempo.
Tenuto	A short line over or under a note means to play *Tenuto*. Give the note extra emphasis, holding it for its full value.
Tie	A **Tie** is a curved line that connects two notes of the same pitch. Hold one sound for the combined value of both notes.
Tone	A **Tone** is the distance from one key to another, higher or lower, black or white, with one key in between.
Transposition	Playing music written in one key in a different key is called **Transposition**.
Triplets	A **Quaver Triplet** fills the time of one crotchet.
Vivace	*Vivace* means "lively."
Upbeat (Pick-up)	A note that comes before the first full bar is called an **Upbeat**.

AD LIBS 8, 12, 25, 29, 66, 67, 79

ARPEGGIOS
A Minor, 25
C, F, and G Major, 11
Summary, 104–107

CHORDS IN CLOSE POSITION
A Minor, 26
C Major, 23
D Minor, 85
E Minor, 69
F Major, 80
G Major, 52
Summary, 104–107

FAKING IT 24, 55, 77

FIVE-FINGER PATTERNS
A Minor, 25
C Major/A Minor, 29
F Major, 11
F Major/D Minor, 79
G Major/E Minor, 67

MUSIC THEORY 27

REPERTOIRE
A Minor Tango, 26
All the Pretty Little Horses, 50
Allegro (Gurlitt), 48
Allegro, from "A Little Night Music," 60
Arabesque, 90
At the End of the Day, 98
Band on the Beach, 41
Baroque Boogie, 62
Beautiful Brown Eyes, 24
Blues for a Count, 65
Changing Lanes, 42
Chorale, 13
Close By, 23
Dixieland Jam, 9
The Entertainer, 100
Etude (Schytte), 49
Etude (Duvernoy), 64
Für Elise, 102
Humoresque, 28
Hush, Little Baby, 55
Jig, 34
Joshua Fit the Battle of Jericho, 56

Latin Logic, 86
Lullaby Angel, 32
Lyrical Prelude, 96
Michael, Row the Boat Ashore, 55
Midnight Snack Attack, 12
Mister Banjo, 68
Morning Bells, 16
On Cloud Nine, 10
On the Bridge at Twilight, 58
On the Prowl, 69
A Pleasant Morning, 81
Ready to Rock!, 52
Rhapsody, 72
Ribbons, 18
Rondeau, 43
Rustic Dance, 30
Scarborough Fair, 31
Six Ate Beets, 82
Song Without Words, 54
Spanish Dance, 53
Symphony No. 9 (Dvořák), 76–77
Take It Easy, 14
A Tender Moment, 88
Too Good to Be Tuba, 20
Turkish March, 6
Two-Four-Six-Eight, 36
Wade in the Water, 74
Walking the Beat, 44
Wandering, 75
Wayfaring Stranger, 22
The Winter Wind, 92
You Can't Lose with the Blues, 7

SCALES, CHORD PROGRESSIONS, and PRIMARY CHORDS
Key of A Minor, 47
Key of C Major, 39
Key of D Minor, 85
Key of E Minor, 71
Key of F Major, 80
Key of G Major, 51
Summary, 104–107

SIGHT READING 40, 94

TECHNIQUE TIPS 11, 16, 26, 38, 64

STYLE CLIPS 77, 78

QUICK-LICKS 8, 15, 66, 95